NEW YORK'S 50 BEST

—

Places to Find Peace and Quiet

Allan Ishac

CITY & COMPANY
New York

City & Company
22 West 23rd Street
New York, NY 10010

Printed in the United States of America

Design by Nancy Steiny Design

Library of Congress Cataloging-in-Publication Data
is available upon request.

ISBN 1-885492-16-2

Publisher's Note
Neither City & Company nor the author has any
interest, financial or personal, in the locations listed
in this book. No fees were paid or services rendered
in exchange for inclusion in these pages.
Please also note that every effort was made to ensure
that information regarding phone numbers, hours,
admission fees, and transit routes was accurate and
up-to-date at the time of publication.

Acknowledgments
Sincere thanks to Susan Golomb, my agent, who has
a wonderful gift for handling the business of writing,
so I can sit back and relax. And to everyone at City
and Company, but most especially to Nancy Steiny
and Jillian Blume Griggs, and Kristin Frederickson.

Dedication

To my family—for loving me even when peace

and quiet are the farthest things from my mind.

Contents

~

Introduction

I like peace and quiet.
I also think they may be essential to
good health and a happy mind.
In a city that seems to offer everything,
however, peace and quiet are rare
indeed. It's hard to find even a
moment's respite from the cacophony
of assaulting sounds: blaring car horns
and clattering garbage trucks, ringing
phones and noisy neighbors, the
thunder of the subway, the scream
of urgent sirens.

As New Yorkers, we learn to tune out
the offensive din, but it takes great
effort and exacts a weighty toll.
Noise, more prevalent than any
pollution we face in this city, can make
us tired, irritable—and even ill.

So how can we stay and still get away?
It's a question I've been asking
myself for a long time, and
New York's 50 Best Places to Find
Peace and Quiet is the answer.
This is a guide to urban sanctuaries,
wonderful places I've discovered
throughout the city that offer
relaxation and refuge. Some are
outdoors; some are in. Some charge
a fee; most are free.
What they all have in common is
that they offer rest and retreat—a
refreshing dip into an oasis of solitude.
I hope you'll carry this guide with
you in your briefcase, backpack, or
handbag and remember it when you
need to escape to a tranquil place—even
for just a minute—or an hour—in your
otherwise hectic day.

Allan Ishac
New York City

Abigail
Adams Smith
Museum

Address: 421 E. 61st St. bet. First & York Aves.
Phone: 838-6878
Hours: Monday through Friday, Noon to 4 P.M.;
Sunday from September to May, 1 P.M. to 5 P.M.;
Tuesday in June and July, 5:30 P.M. to 8 P.M.;
closed in August
Admission: $3
Subway: 4, 5, 6 to 59th St., walk east
Bus: M15 (First and Second Aves.); M5 (57th
St. crosstown) to First Ave., walk north.

When you walk through the gates of this charming museum, you enter more than a peaceful enclave—you pass into another era.

Constructed in 1799, this former coach house is one of only eight surviving eighteenth century buildings in Manhattan still open to the public. Its relationship to Abigail herself (daughter of second U.S. president, John Adams) is tenuous; she never actually lived here, but it was part of a country estate she owned. After a stint as a riverfront hotel in the 1820s, the handsome stone house was used as a private residence, then suffered through decades of neglect. Finally, in 1924, the stone house was purchased and restored by The Colonial Dames of America, who filled the museum's nine rooms with furniture and artifacts of the Federal period. For the price of admission the tour is well worth taking; however, I found the museum's most cloistered attraction to be the reconstructed eighteenth century garden. You access the backyard garden simply by walking around the museum, and once you pay for the tour, the kindly docents will let you sit back there all day among the precisely planted flora and colorful perennials.

You can also climb the steps in the northwest corner of the garden to a particularly peaceful upper terrace, where there's a natural schist outcropping (the same Manhattan stone quarried to build the museum), ideal for spring and summer sunning.

Bartow-Pell Mansion Museum

Address: 895 Shore Road, Bronx
Phone: (718) 885-1461
Hours: Museum open Wednesday, Saturday and
Sunday, Noon to 4 P.M.; grounds open Tuesday
through Sunday, 8:30 A.M. to 4:30 P.M.
Admission: $2.50 for museum tour;
grounds free
Subway: 6 to Pelham Bay stop, then take bus
Bus: 45 Westchester-Bee Line to gates
(no bus Sundays)
Auto: Call for directions

About once a month, I contract a serious case of city claustrophobia, for which I know only one cure—trees, grass, open space. And lots of it. On days like these, when even Central Park lacks adequate healing power, I head Bronx bound to the Bartow-Pell Mansion, where I can find ample doses of the much needed antidotes.

Although located near the Westchester border, Bartow-Pell is surprisingly accessible. Looking into the winding drive and wooded compound

from this pillared entranceway, a splendid antici-
pation of the country elegance lying ahead
envelops you.

The mansion itself, one of the finest examples of
early Federal-style architecture in the country, is
famous for its sea-shell shaped, three-story
hanging staircase; don't miss this gravity-defying
marvel of construction. The self-guided tour
also leads to a pleasant "orangerie"—the French
name for a sun-room—where strong southern
light warms the chilliest of winter days.

Outside, explore the mansion's nine-and-a-half
rolling acres, including the four-tiered formal
garden which seems to spill into the nearby
Long Island Sound. The claustrophobia cure
reaches full potency after you've walked the
property's well-marked paths through unspoiled
forests and marshlands, then venture out to the
bordering Siwanoy Hiking Trail through more
than two thousand acres of Pelham Bay Park.

Battery Park

Address: Battery Place and State St.
Hours: Daily, 8 A.M. to 1 A.M.
Admission: Free
Subway: R to Battery Park; 6 to Bowling
Green; 1 to South Ferry
Bus: M1, 6 (Broadway) to State St.

this park at the southern tip of Manhattan has served as an inviting public space for more than 200 years, and is still a qualified haven from the pressures of the nearby financial district.

Named for the battery of cannons originally placed here to guard Manhattan (an early nineteenth century fort—Castle Clinton—still remains and now serves as ticket office for Ellis Island and the Statue of Liberty), Battery Park is a spacious and breezy memorial to all those brave souls who have protected our shores. You'll find plenty of sun and seagulls, a wide riverfront esplanade, inspiring water views, and perhaps the most deeply affecting monument in

our city—the drowning scene depicted in the
partially submerged American Merchant
Mariner's Memorial (north end of the park).
I would venture that at some point we have all
reached out in this kind of desperation.

There are miles of pleasant pathways lined with
park benches, too, and grass you can actually sit
on. For more privacy, I retire to the shadow of
the eight stone monoliths comprising the East
Coast War Memorial. There always seems to be
a free bench here, even at lunch hour when over-
stressed Wall Streeters stream into the park to
regain composure and perspective.

*Traveler's Note: Near the southernmost
end of the park is the entrance to the
Staten Island Ferry—at fifty cents for a
50-minute round-trip cruise, this is still the
best way to see the glittering Lower Manhattan
skyline. And, during off-peak hours, it can
be mighty peaceful, too.*

The **Bell Tower** at Riverside **Church**

Address: 490 Riverside Drive at 120th St.
Phone: 222-5900
Hours: Sunday, 12:30 P.M. to 4 P.M.;
Weekday hours vary, call ahead.
Admission: $1
Subway: 1, B, C to 116th St., walk northeast
Bus: M104 (Broadway) to 116th St.

n ow I know why Quasimodo took refuge in a bell tower—it must have been the privacy, the views, the romantic promise, and those great big beautiful bells.

✠

At 392 feet, this Gothic belfry is one of the world's tallest, offering some nifty, unobstructed views of New York and New Jersey. It also houses seventy-four memorable carillon bells, a gift of the Rockefeller family, which range in size from a twenty-ton bronze monster—still the largest and heaviest tuned bell ever cast—to a dainty ten-pounder. The total weight of the bells exceeds one hundred tons, a tremendous stress load which called for some of the most concentrated steel reinforcement ever used in a skyscraper.

✠

Purchase your ticket at the visitor's center; take a quick elevator ride; then climb another 147 steps through the maze of bells to the narrow, outdoor observation platform (carry a sweater—it's windy up here). In all my visits to the bell tower, I've rarely encountered another living soul (no dead ones either). Be aware, however, that the year-round Sunday carillon recitals do attract a small crowd of appreciative—but perhaps slightly crazed— pilgrims looking for a good head ringing.

✠

The bell tower is worth a special trip from anywhere—it's way up in the heavens, giddily inspiring, and when the bells toll on the quarter hour, you can scream as loud as you want without being arrested.

The **Boathouse** in **Central Park**

Address: Enter at 72nd St. and Fifth Ave.,
walk 200 yards north
Phone: 517-2233
Hours: Monday through Friday,
10:30 A.M. to 5:30 P.M.; Saturday and
Sunday, 10 A.M. to 6 P.M. (seasonal)
Admission: $10 per hour per boat
(seats up to five)
Subway: 6 to 68th St., walk west
Bus: M1, 2, 3, 4
(Fifth and Madison Aves. to 72nd St.)

Y ou're skimming through tranquil waters passing below a nineteenth century wooden footbridge. You see a flock of water birds in the distance as another small boat emerges from a reed bed nearby. Is this a fishing pond in Maine? An unexplored inlet off Chesapeake Bay? Would you believe the Central Park lake?

Even veteran New Yorkers have been known to mistake a picturesque and placid city refuge for an overcrowded, off-limits tourist trap. While the Central Park lake does draw large crowds on weekends, it offers weekday visitors a unique and inexpensive way to escape the city without ever leaving it.

Purchase your ticket at the fast food counter in the Loeb Boathouse Cafeteria. Courteous attendants will then assist you with oars (and requisite life jacket), and set you off in your own rowboat. Wherever you can row you can go, and with more than eighteen acres of open water and side pools, you can go far.
This is one place where I guarantee you won't be bugged or bothered, badgered or bullied. In fact, no one can reach you even if they want to. Which is reason enough to go row.

Traveler's Note: Romantics can inquire at the Loeb Boathouse about spring and summer gondola rides on the lake ($30 for a half-hour).

Books
& Co.

Address: 939 Madison Ave. at 74th St.
Phone: 737-1450
Hours: Monday through Saturday, 10 A.M. to
6 P.M.; Sunday, Noon to 5 P.M.
Admission: Free
Subway: 6 to 77th St, walk west
Bus: M1, 2, 3, 4, 18
(Fifth and Madison Aves.) to 75th St.

this is the bookstore I'd been searching for
all my life: exposed brick walls lined
floor to ceiling with mahogany bookcases; long
center tables piled high with tempting
titles; a cheery chesterfield couch where I could
read three chapters of a relished novel
before deciding to buy; a sympathetic staff that
believes the words of great writers ought
to be lingered over, not rushed through.

Brimming with fine literature, unusual and
out-of-print books, plus a superb collection of
books on art, Books & Co. feels as

though it were plucked whole from a London
back alley and deposited quietly on
Madison Avenue. This is an old-fashioned
bookstore, a browser's paradise, a comfy,
cluttered place where the disarray seems an
integral part of the homey atmosphere.
Owner Jeannette Watson uses her clever theme
windows and Tuesday night author readings
(photographs of the visiting literary luminaries
line the walls of the first floor staircase)
to further cultivate the inviting milieu.
Wear a watch—you're in constant
danger of losing entire afternoons among
the entrancing and enticing tomes.

Books & Co. is so rare, so familiar, so special,
a number of its clients actually wrote a
commemorative book about it.
I quote:
"It is a haven, a heaven, a place where
the human spirit is revived each time the
threshold is passed."
Need I say another word?

Carapan

**Address: 5 West 16th St., garden level,
bet. Fifth and Sixth Aves.
Phone: 633-6220
Hours: Daily, 10 A.M. to 9:30 P.M. by appt.
Admission: Half-hour sessions, $42.50;
One-hour sessions, $75
Subway: 4, 5, 6, N, R to Union Square
Bus: M2, 3, 4, 5 (Fifth Ave.) to 16th St.**

It may cost a little more for the peace and quiet they offer at Carapan, but, to me, it is worth the price.

A place where you go for bodywork, both esoteric and familiar, Carapan offers everything from Swedish massage and shiatsu to aromatherapy treatments and herbal facials. I can tell you from first-hand experience (pun intended) that the massage practitioners here are first-rate, with special attention given to those parts of the body especially vulnerable to Big City stress.

I can also assure you that you will return

to Carapan as much for the healing
atmosphere as the healing arts.

As soon as you walk into Carapan, you
can feel its revitalizing effects. The
subtle scents and calming energy of the
Southwest have been flawlessly re-created
here; juniper, piñon, and mesquite incense
burn; soothing music plays; and you are
instantly transported from the outskirts
of Greenwich Village to the mesas of
Santa Fe. Even their gift shop evokes
the spirit of the region, with an intriguing
assortment of Native American offerings
from sage smudge sticks to feathered
"dream catchers."

Carapan calls itself a tranquil place
where you can go to restore your spirit.
I call it that and much more.
Even if you don't go for the bodywork,
stop by just to inhale.

The Cloisters

Address: Northern tip of Fort Tryon Park
Phone: 923-3700
Hours: Tuesday through Sunday, 9:30 A.M. to 5:15 P.M.;
closed Monday
Admission: $7 suggested donation
Subway: A to 190th St, walk north
Bus: M4 directly to The Cloisters
Auto: Henry Hudson Pkwy. north to first
exit after George Washington Bridge

I was running along a treacherous rampart, chased by a frothing gargoyle...I came to the arched doorway of a remote abbey where I was offered refuge by an employee of the Metropolitan Museum of Art...

Was this a dream or just vivid imagery from a trip to The Cloisters? Built exclusively to house art from the Middle Ages, this extension of the Metropolitan Museum of Art is almost *too* medieval. Gregorian chants fill the air; people shuffle past through darkened,

vaulted passageways...I felt a disconcerting and
disorienting urge to don monk's robes
and shave my head.

The supreme serenity of this hilltop monastery
is always an inspirational treat. When
John D. Rockefeller Jr. built The Cloisters
in 1938, he even purchased a tract of land
across the river to preserve the arcadian views.
Then he shipped original architectural
elements from five cloisters in France to be
the centerpieces of this medieval world high
above the Hudson. Everything here—from
the magnificent tapestries and period
colonnades to the cobblestoned courtyards
and outdoor herb garden—is designed to
evoke the mood of thirteenth century Europe.
And it works.

If you're a fan of time travel, just board the
A train for this mysterious medieval world.
P.S. The gargoyles are harmless.

Conservatory Garden

Address: 105th St. and Fifth Ave.
Hours: Daily; 8 A.M. to Dusk
Admission: Free
Subway: 6 to 103rd St., walk west
Bus: M1, 2, 3, 4
(Fifth or Madison Aves.) to 105th St.

The Conservatory Garden may be the best kept secret in Manhattan. New York's only formal garden stands elegantly at 105th Street and Fifth Avenue across from the Museum of the City of New York. This is uncharted territory for many residents and visitors who haven't yet discovered the city's attractions above 96th Street. What are you waiting for?

The six-acre garden is perfectly safe, in addition to being one of the few official "Quiet Zones" in this city that actually is. When you enter the huge wrought iron gates, you'll immediately think you've stepped into the sweeping backyard of a

stately English home. There are precisely
trimmed hedges, enchanted arbor walkways,
ornate flower beds, sculpted fountains, and one of
the most spectacular pergolas you will ever see—
all tidily organized in the Victorian tradition.

The south end, also called The Secret Garden
as a tribute to the Frances Hodgson Burnett
children's classic, seems always to be filled
with endless birdsong. It has particular charm
with its playful fountain, hidden niches, and
bountiful flower beds.

*Traveler's Note: Five blocks north through the
park, landscape architect Laura Starr and The
Central Park Conservancy have transformed the
Harlem Meer (Dutch for "lake") from a swampy
soup of algae and garbage into a stunning
showcase with wetlands and a sandy beach.
The new Dana Discovery Center, at shore's
edge, offers a free program of hands-on science
projects and fishing for city kids. It's all free.*

Dia
Center Rooftop

Address: 548 W. 22nd St.
bet. Tenth and Eleventh Aves.
Phone: 989-5912/ 431-9232
Hours: Thursday through Sunday,
Noon to 6 P.M., closed July and August
Admission: $2 suggested donation
Subway: A, C, E to 23rd St., walk west
Bus: M11 (Tenth Ave.) to 23rd St.

there is something about being on a rooftop in New York that inevitably evokes feelings of magic and romance.

Perhaps it's those unforgettable silver-screen images of Marlon Brando in ON THE WATERFRONT with his loft-loving pigeons, or WEST SIDE STORY's moon-lit passion between Tony and Maria. Whatever it is, I do know that standing high above the city with nothing but a cloudless sky overhead is infinitely liberating. They seem to know it at the

Dia Center for the Arts, too. The Dia Center's 35,000-square-foot facility is famous for introducing emerging contemporary artists through full-floor, long-term exhibitions. This unusual arrangement allows visitors to ponder art in an open, unconfined setting.

Sculptor Dan Graham has contributed a stunning glass and metal configuration for the rooftop that is, in itself, a "reflective" experience. A thirty-six-foot glass square surrounds a smaller circle of glass. When the observer steps into the sculpture (participation is encouraged), it is a multisensory adventure. The Graham piece is well-integrated into a roof deck park with benches and trees. There is also a small concession stand.

While the Dia Center rooftop may not sit on the city's tallest building, it does offer a remote roosting place for safety and solitude above the mean streets.

Equitable Tower Atrium

Address: 787 Seventh Ave.
bet. 51st and 52nd Sts.
Hours: Daily, 10 A.M. to 6 P.M.
Admission: Free
Subway: N, R to 49th St.; 1 or 9 to 50th St.
Bus: M6, 7 (Seventh Ave.) to 51st St.

a few years back the city began offering generous financial incentives to buildings that provided public atriums, plazas, and open spaces. Developers responded with a contrasting mix of macabre, mall-like settings and truly magnificent retreats.

One of the best is inside the Equitable Atrium, where they've hidden a gift of solitude: a forty-foot, semicircular marble settee. This arching bench is a sculptural, spatial, and acoustical phenomenon. I will never understand how it works, but take just a few steps inside this skylit crescent and you have the sensation of

being held firmly in a protective marble cocoon.
Add the matching flora-filled fountain and dense
screen of tropical conifers, and it becomes
nearly impossible to leave this gentle embrace.

From inside this benevolent bench enclosure
note Roy Lichtenstein's "Mural with Blue
Brushstroke" dominating the wall behind.
It was painted on site in 1984 and is one of
the celebrated artist's largest works.

Here are other public spaces I rate highly:
Crystal Pavilion (Third Avenue and 50th
Street): The stainless steel decor is a tad cold,
but two shimmering water walls on the lower
level warm things up. Continental Atrium
(Maiden Lane and Front Street): The intricate
Tinker Toy interior is a playful place to relax.
J.P. Morgan Building (60 Wall Street): With a
trickling fountain and ample seating the
galleria is a receptive retreat for perusing
the Wall Street Journal.

Erol Beker
Chapel
in St. Peter's Church

Address: Lexington Ave. at 54th St.
Phone: 935-2200
Hours: Daily, 7 A.M. to 9 P.M.
Admission: Free
Subway: 6 to 51st St.
Bus: M101, M102 (Lexington and Third Aves.)
to 51st St.

What if you owned a tiny parcel of land in the center of Manhattan, and you had an insatiable appetite for peace and quiet? And what if you decided to transform that sliver of land into your own corner of celestial calm, a hushed and happy place where acclaimed American sculptor Louise Nevelson agreed to do the interior design?

Well, I'm guessing it would look and feel a whole lot like the inviolate surroundings of the Erol Beker Chapel—as much an

exuberant work of modern art as a dulcet
haven for heart and soul.

This is Ms. Nevelson's only permanent
sculptural environment in New York City, and
she wanted the unique prayer space, tucked
inside the north wall of St. Peter's Church (the
jagged appendage at the base of the Citicorp
complex), to exude purity. That's why
everything in this twenty-eight by twenty-one
foot, five-sided chapel is white: White painted
sculptural elements on white walls; white
floors; white altar; and white pews. Even its
one window is frosted white.

I am unable to pass within five blocks of this
thumb-sized peace pocket without its
enthralling gravity drawing me in. The
stillness here is extraordinary. Just gaze into
the solitary sanctuary lamp for a minute
and you'll return to the streets a more
agreeable human being.

The Flower Garden at W. 91st Street

Address: Riverside Park at 91st St.
Hours: Daily, 24 Hours
Admission: Free
Subway: 1, 9 to 86th St., walk northwest
Bus: M5 (Riverside Drive) to 91st St.

When Upper Westsiders talk about their garden, they're usually referring to the flower garden at 91st Street in Riverside Park.

❧

While not a community garden per se, local residents attend to virtually all aspects of its planting and upkeep, and do an exceptional job. The fenced flower beds— about one-hundred yards west of Riverside Drive—are not only beautiful, their grandeur seems to quiet minds and mouths. Sit along the benches surrounding the garden and you'll notice that conversations are muted, apparently hushed out of respect for the blooming orchestra of natural splendor. The garden's fragrant cul-de-sac, situated within a knoll of dogwoods which bloom spectacularly in the spring, is also the turnaround point for a broad esplanade favored by joggers and bikers.

❧❦☙

The esplanade, providing elevated views of the Hudson River, is divided by a wide grass island and runs to 83rd Street. I have photographs of my father walking along this exact stretch of Riverside Park in the 1940s, which must prove that the desire to find peace and quiet in New York is a genetic predisposition.

❧❦☙

Traveler's Note: One-hundred-fifty feet above the garden and two blocks south is the Soldiers and Sailors Monument, another wonderful spot for peaceful repose. This huge circular monument has massive marble and concrete terraces overlooking Riverside Park and New Jersey, with the kind of broad stone benches you'll feel compelled to sprawl out upon.

Ford Foundation Building

Address: 320 East 43rd St.
bet. First and Second Aves.
Phone: 573-5000
Hours: Monday through Friday, 9 A.M. to 5 P.M.
Admission: Free
Subway: 4, 5, 6 to Grand Central, walk east
Bus: M15 (First and Second Aves.) to 42nd St.;
M104 or M42 crosstown to Second Ave.

In a stroke of architectural genius, the designer of the Ford Foundation—Kevin Roche—put the building around the park, instead of the park around the building. Here you can enjoy a 160-foot high, glass-walled, third-of-an-acre terraced garden, lushly landscaped with exotic greenery all year round.

Since there are no formal benches or chairs here, and no food or drinks allowed, Roche's towering greenhouse plaza does not draw the kind of crowds other public spaces seem to

attract. In fact, the rainforest-like setting
is almost always unoccupied.

You'll be most comfortable ascending to the east
side of the top tier, where you'll find a three-foot,
sun-drenched sitting wall, a quiet vantage point
from which to study the seventeen full-grown
trees (including acacia, magnolia, and eucalyptus),
999 shrubs, 148 vines, and 21,954 ground cover
plants. The landscapers also rotate special plant-
ings for each season with tulips in spring,
begonias in summer, chrysanthemums in fall and
poinsettias in winter. The three levels of garden
court are lined with brick pathways descending
to a still-water pool, which gratefully accepts your
coins on behalf of UNICEF (appropriate with the
United Nations located just half a block east).

At the Ford Foundation the air is dense with the
earthy scent of bursting horticulture, a kind of
intoxicating chlorophyll panacea guaranteed
to calm the most hyperactive minds.

The Frick Collection

Address: 1 East 70th St. at Fifth Ave.
Phone: 288-0700
Hours: Tuesday through Saturday, 10 A.M. to 6 P.M.;
Sunday, 1 to 6 P.M.;
closed Monday
Admission: $5
Subway: 6 to 68th St., walk west
Bus: M1, 2, 3, 4
(Fifth and Madison Aves.) to 68th St.

I think it's the frogs that make the Frick.

That might sound odd until you visit the
former mansion of Henry Clay Frick, now
the home to one of New York's unique art
collections. Enter on 70th Street and walk
straight back to the skylit Garden Court.
That's where you'll see two frisky frogs,
perpetually spouting water at each other
from either end of a long center fountain.

I've always found this water play to be
mesmerizing, and the planted Garden Court,

with its polished floors and marble benches,
to be immeasurably soothing.

The Frick's residential setting and unhurried
ambience are ideal for viewing the formidable
art collection, including some of the best known
European paintings by artists like Velazquez,
Van Dyck, Vermeer, El Greco, and Goya.
Most of the museum's rooms are lit by overhead
skylights, including the West Gallery where
I defy any mortal man or woman to sit on the
ample sofas facing one of Rembrandt's
spectacularly famous self-portraits and not feel
overcome by the sublime beauty. One minor
rub: Like me, you'll probably ache to get out
on the west portico and elegant outdoor
terraces. Unfortunately, they're inexplicably
(and forever) closed to the public.

So, you'll have to settle for the frogs.

The General
Theological
Seminary

Address: 175 Ninth Ave. bet. 20th and 21st St.
Phone: 243-5150
Hours: Monday through Friday, Noon to 3 P.M.;
Saturday 11:30 A.M. to 3 P.M.;
closed Sunday
Admission: Free
Subway: A, C, E to 23rd St.; 1 to 18th St.
Bus: M11 (Ninth and Tenth Aves.) to 23rd St.

Combine the pastoral serenity of a New England campus quad with the cloistered formality of an English collegiate close, and you'll know just what it feels like to visit the seminary of the Episcopal Church in Chelsea.

Your first reaction upon entering the pristine grounds (you must sign in at the Ninth Avenue entrance) is utter disbelief that they even open this space to the public—it really is that special. But the

seminarians here are extraordinarily nice
people who want to contribute to
their community, and have generously
done so with this outdoor peace offering.
They'll even greet a visitor's naive questions
about the seminary's exquisite architecture
with a polite and patient smile...
(it's nineteenth century Gothic Revival).

The red brick buildings which frame the
seminary grounds were built beginning in
1836 and cover an entire city block. The
complex is also a registered National
Historic Landmark. Don't miss the Chapel
of the Good Shepherd at the heart of the
block-long quad. It's a charming, simple,
country-like chapel that glows with the
warmth of beautiful stained glass and
dark, rich wood carvings. After strolling
the landscaped pathways of the seminary's
outer yard, I've always found the chapel
an ideal place to explore my own
inner pathways.

Greenacre Park

**Address: 221 East 51st St.
bet. Second and Third Aves.
Hours: Daily, 8 A.M. to 6 P.M.
Admission: Free
Subway: E or F to 53rd St.;
6 to 51st St., walk east.
Bus: M101 (Lexington and
Third Aves.) to 51st St.**

While this vest-pocket park in the heart of
the East Midtown commercial and residential
district is nowhere near an acre, it does offer
an acre's worth of rare tranquility.

Like Paley Park, its smaller cousin a few
blocks away on East 53rd Street, Greenacre
Park boasts a dramatic two-story waterfall,
this one constructed of massive granite blocks.
There's a babbling brook here, too, which
ambles along the east wall and feeds into a
plunge pool. The intermingling sounds
of gurgling, flowing, and cascading water
significantly reduce street noise, insulating

this very pleasant park from the
incessant tug of the city.

I particularly recommend the park on rainy
days when you can ponder the waterfalls
alone, undisturbed, and comfortably dry
under the trellis roof of the west terrace,
where you'll find plenty of outdoor chairs
and tables. In good weather, however,
Greenacre Park is no place to linger
during weekday lunch hours because
local business people swarm here to soak
in the sun and quiet. The park brochure
says it was designed "to provide a place
for the general public to gain special
repose from the increasing city experience
of noise, concrete, and humdrum."
Makes me feel like humming just
thinking about it.

Green-Wood Cemetery

Address: Fifth Ave. at 25th St., Brooklyn
Phone: (718) 768-7300
Hours: Daily, 8 A.M. to 4 P.M.
Admission: Free
Subway: N, R to 25th St., walk east
Auto: Brooklyn Battery Tunnel onto
the Brooklyn-Queens Expressway (BQE),
to Third Ave. exit,
left on 25th St. to Fifth Ave.

i want you to forget for a moment that there are 500,000 dead people here.

Consider instead that this rural cemetery was designed in 1838 by Frederick Law Olmsted as a pastoral park with rolling hills, five lakes, thirty miles of serpentine pathways, and some of the the city's oldest trees—all in a quiescent setting (478 acres) half the size of Central Park.

Within this bucolic, sepulchral masterpiece

situated at the highest point in Brooklyn you'll find no cars, no trucks, no subways, no sirens, no screaming kids—and virtually no people. The profound stillness here is, well, a lot like what you'd find at a cemetery.

For me, great cemeteries have always been places to stroll with a trusted friend. Green-Wood has the additional appeal of its celebrity occupants, among whom are stained-glass master Louis Comfort Tiffany, pencil man Eberhard Faber, piano maker Henry Steinway, and soap magnate William Colgate. And I discovered why Green-Wood Cemetery has a particularly magical air. This is the eternal resting place of actor Frank Morgan. You know...the Wizard of Oz.

Traveler's Note: A walking tour of the famous monuments by ex-policeman and Green-Wood buff, John Cashman, is conducted on Sundays in the spring and fall for a nominal fee. Call ahead for times and gathering location.

High Tea
at the
Villard House

Address: 457 Madison Ave.
bet. 50th and 51st Sts.
Phone: 888-7000
Hours: Daily, 2 P.M. to 5 P.M.
Admission: $19.50 per person
Subway: E or F to 53rd St. and Madison Ave.
Bus: M1, 2, 3, 4
(Fifth and Madison Aves.) to 50th St.

If everyone in New York were required to
break for afternoon tea, I'm sure we'd all feel a
bit more civilized and a lot less harried.

This dignified ritual is celebrated in
grand European style at a number of
midtown hotels. Having sampled several
in pursuit of the serenity and sophistication
customarily associated with this rite,
I personally prefer teatime in the Villard
House at The New York Palace Hotel.

Enter through the courtyard of this former
nineteenth century mansion, walk to
the right side of the grand staircase, and
proceed to the secluded Gold Room
—an ornately decorated parlor
with a dozen handsomely set tables.

The lights are dim; the pastries
are sublime; the service is extremely
cordial; and you'll be lulled into a mellow
mood by the mellifluous sounds
of a lovely harp. Because the three-course
traditional afternoon tea is somewhat
expensive here, you might want to reserve
this experience for an unusual and
unpressured first date (guaranteed to
warm the cockles of anyone who joins you),
or for the perfect way to end
a hectic midtown workday.

Inwood Hill Park

Address: 207th St. and Seaman Ave.
Hours: Daily, 24 hours
Admission: Free
Subway: A, 1, 9 to 207th St.
Bus: M100 (Amsterdam Ave.) to 207th St.

When I was a child, my family home bordered a large, wooded nature preserve. From my bedroom window, this endless forest seemed a dark, dangerous place. But as I grew older, it became a friend—a world to wander aimlessly, an alone place to conjure grand visions, or to cry, openly and unobserved.

I have been able to reconnect with that secret forest of my childhood at Inwood Hill Park. This beautiful, rustic, rocky park is the largest expanse of natural woodland left in Manhattan. You can walk along miles of meandering pathways within its 196 acres, or blaze your own trails over mossy glens, fallen trees, and sparse underbrush. Flag down one of the regularly-patrolling Urban Park Rangers to secure a quaint, hand-drawn trail map.

Inwood Park holds two special surprises: The mysterious Indian Caves that remain largely undisturbed (you'll find them at the center of the park, near Pothole Road on the trail map), and the narrow ledges overhanging the Hudson. To access the ledges, follow the fence along the western edge of the park until you find the rolled-back fence openings. Here you can shimmy through to the most scenic picnicking spot in the city. Historians will note the marked boulder where it is believed Peter Minuit bought Manhattan Island from the Reckgawawanc Indians for trinkets and beads worth about 60 Dutch guilders.

Traveler's Note: As with all city parks, it is prudent to make your visits during the day, and with a companion.

Isamu Noguchi
Garden Museum

Address: 32-37 Vernon Blvd.,
Long Island City, Queens
Phone: (718) 204-7088
Hours: Wednesday, Saturday, Sunday
11 A.M. to 6 P.M., April through November
Admission: $4 suggested donation
Subway: N to Broadway (Long Island City),
walk west nine blocks to Vernon Blvd.,
south two blocks to museum
Shuttle Bus: Leaves Saturday and Sunday
from Asia Society; call for times

Isamu Noguchi was so patient with the development of a sculpture, he would sometimes study a piece of raw marble or granite for years before making the first strike. He called this process "discovering the stone's essence."

At the Isamu Noguchi Garden Museum, I could almost feel the master artist urging me to take up my own inner sculpting tools— to split and cut, chisel and polish—to discover the essence of self. Noguchi's sculptures speak this personally and deeply.

Forming the eye of the storm in Long Island City, this dignified, uncluttered, unexpectedly tranquil gallery and Zen garden contain more than 300 Noguchi sculptures of stone, wood and clay (as well as his rice paper and wire Akari light sculptures), each placed with precision and sensitivity to elicit the most profound reaction. The peace of his rock garden alone, enjoyed also by a family of doves, far outweighs any extra effort it might take to get here.

I suggest a day trip, so you'll have time to absorb the illuminating messages Noguchi has chiseled into his oracular boulders; weekend shuttle busses from the Asia Society at 70th Street and Park Avenue ensure an easy journey.

Traveler's Note: Since you're here, walk two blocks north to Socrates Park, a raw, rubble-strewn, riverfront creation that's the home to sculpture on a towering scale.

The Jacqueline Onassis Reservoir Running Path

Address: Mid Central Park, 86th to 96th Sts.
Hours: Daily, 24 hours
Admission: Free
Subway: 4, 5, 6 to 86th St., walk west, to
entrance at 89th St. and Fifth Ave.
Bus: M1, 2, 3, 4 to 86th St.

You've probably heard of "runner's high" —
that state of quasi-euphoria every serious
aerobic athlete encounters. In New York,
we have our own unique version called
"reservoir runner's high." It kicks in with
sweet reliability after a lap or two of the
spectacular reservoir path.

A big body of water like this one (107 acres
at capacity) attracts a large variety of
migrating water fowl, along with the normal
contingent of local mallards and seagulls.
A bridle path also runs parallel to the track

for much of its length, so it's not unusual to find yourself matching strides with an equestrian or two. The combined effect makes a circuit of the elevated, 1.6-mile cinder path the equivalent of jogging the perimeter of a country lake.

You'll encounter other striders along the way, but these are conscientious, quiet athletes. It's a very civilized group. And if you stand by the South Gate House (86th Street, looking due north), you'll see one of my favorite sights in Manhattan—a buildingless horizon. You can cast your gaze far out into the distance from here and behold only water, trees, and flocks of birds. What a relief for your skyscraped eyes.

The picturesque reservoir path is more than a spot for furtive celebrity watching; it's a refreshing island of water in a big stone sea. Drink deeply.

Jacques Marchais
Center of Tibetan Art

Address: 338 Lighthouse Ave., Staten Island
Phone: (718) 987-3478, (718) 987-3500
Hours: April to November,
Wednesday through Sunday, 1 P.M. to 5 P.M.
Admission: $3 adults, $1 children
Bus: From Staten Island Ferry, take S74 to
Lighthouse Ave., then ten minute walk up hill
(allow ninety minutes total from Manhattan)
Auto: Call for directions

This cliff-clinging museum on Staten Island is such an authentic recreation of a Tibetan monastery temple, a group of Buddhist monks actually come here to worship. For them, this is Tibet.

The creation of Jacqueline Klauber, who used the name Jacques Marchais for professional reasons, the museum holds one of the largest collections of Tibetan art outside Tibet. The lamasery altar is so jam-packed with gilded Buddhas, ornate prayer wheels, elaborate incense burners, and startling ritual masks, you'll wonder how peaceful prayer ever happens here...until you let the transforming powers of these sacred objects envelop you.

Located at the highest point on the Eastern seaboard, the Tibetan museum doesn't exactly have Himalayan vistas, but its distant harbor views are venerated locally. On the tranquil patio garden you'll also see huge baboons, trumpeting elephants, and prancing rabbits...all of the stone variety. The goldfish in the lotus pond, however, are real.

See those colorful prayer flags hanging in the trees? It is believed that the wind carries a prayer made on these flags out to the world. So I prayed for more places just like this one.

Traveler's Note: The Center has an extensive calendar of Far Eastern related events. Call for a list.

John Finley Walk at Carl Schurz Park

Address: 84th to 89th St. and East End Ave.
Hours: Daily, dawn to 1 A.M.
Admission: Free
Subway: 4, 5, 6 to 86th St.
Bus: M86 (86th St. crosstown) to York Ave.,
walk east.; M31 (York Ave.) to 86th St.

Carl Schurz Park is one of those places
in the city one might have heard of but
can't quite pinpoint.

Apparently a lot of city residents and
visitors have trouble pinpointing it because it
remains an unhurried hideaway, ideal for
peace-seekers and slow strollers.
To access this smallish (10.3 acre)
neighborhood park and the John Finley Walk,
climb the broad circular stairs at the 86th
Street entrance until you reach the
raised promenade.

Once there, you can amble along past Gracie Mansion absorbing the history of the century-old, panoramic, and unusually safe park (Hizzoner's house is on the property, so it's well guarded). This is a park for young families and elderly people who gather to enjoy sweeping views of the East River and Roosevelt Island. It's particularly breathtaking at night when river bridges are brightly lit, throwing luminous reflections off the water.

There's a children's playground at the south end where it can get noisy. For optimum privacy, walk north along the promenade past the tall flagpole to where the footpath narrows. Continue for another 100 feet (if you reach the fireboat house you've gone too far) and settle yourself down on a shaded bench. You'll know when you've reached the right place by that telltale sound— the sound of silence.

La Casa Day Spa Floatation

**Address: 41 East 20th St.
bet. Park Ave. and Broadway
Phone: 673-2272
Hours: Monday through Friday
10 A.M. to 8:30 P.M.;
Saturday 10 A.M. to 5:30 P.M.,
closed Sunday
Admission: $50 for one hour float
Subway: 4, 5, 6 to 23rd St.
Bus: M101 (Park Ave., uptown, and Third
Ave., downtown) to 20th St.**

You're naked. Your body is completely relaxed. You're floating weightlessly in your own private sea, a warm, silky liquid rocking you into a state of suspended tranquility.

It's probably safe to say that the last time you experienced this level of bliss was at the threshold of your current incarnation—the womb. Unless, perhaps, you're a "floater."

At this very professional day spa and floatation center they maintain a state-of-the-art floatation room with adjoining private shower. All you bring is your overtaxed body. Begin by decompressing in La Casa's tastefully appointed "tropical" reception area, then get ready to climb into ten inches of water so thoroughly infused with epsom salts, anything (and anyone) can float.

By adjusting light and music levels, you control the degree of sensory deprivation; the fewer external stimuli, the better. Within seconds your buoyant body releases into the anti-gravity effects and your mind voyage begins.

In this liquid cocoon you'll experience all things good, from profound relaxation to genuine euphoria. Studies even suggest that a two-hour float is more restful than a full night's sleep. Which all adds up to the kind of out-of-body sensation you'll want to dive right into.

Lighthouse Park on Roosevelt Island

Address: Northern tip of Roosevelt Island
Hours: Daily, 24 hours
Admission: Free
Subway: B, Q to Roosevelt Island
Tram: Departs from 59th St.
and Second Ave.

there's nothing like escaping to a quiet island when the city encroaches on your sanity. Especially when this quiet island is only five minutes away.

Unfortunately, few New Yorkers think of Roosevelt Island as a viable getaway. They worry they'll get over there and never get back. Or that the aerial tram will deposit them in the river before it lands them safely on the opposite shore. Dispel all fears: Not only can you get to tranquil Lighthouse Park quickly and safely, you can also buy a sandwich at an island deli; catch a half hour of unobstructed rays; and be back at the office before anyone notices.

The short tram ride ($1.40 each way) is an event in itself. You can see virtually every inch of Manhattan (most of Queens, too) from 250 feet up on the soaring Swiss cable cars. Once you alight on this sliver of land, take the red bus (fare is ten cents) as far north as it travels, then stroll along the island's east side until you reach the park. You'll probably see a few fishermen near the tiny granite lighthouse and not much else. You'll also find a wide lawn, hospitable picnic tables, and an exercise course for those inclined.

For loafers like me, the extent of island activity involves reclining on a grassy ridge counting barges as they glide by.

The New York Botanical Garden

Address: 200th St. at Southern Blvd., Bronx
Phone: (718) 817-8500
Hours: Tuesday through Sunday,
10 A.M. to 6 P.M. (4:00 P.M. Winter)
Admission: $3; parking $4
Train: Metro North (Harlem Line) from
Grand Central to Botanical Garden stop
Auto: Henry Hudson Pkwy. to Exit 24,
Moshulu Pkwy. to Botanical Garden exit,
turn right on Southern Blvd., to gardens

Your sense of smell is the most acute sense you have, a fact which makes a trip to the New York Botanical Garden one of the most sensuous experiences there is.

With 250 quiet acres of blooming, burgeoning, bursting gardens, plus the spectacular turn-of-the-century conservatory, this is a seasonless feast for the olfactory palate. The clever horticulturalists here have carefully planned a succession of flowers and

foliage that keep the vast site in almost full
color and fragrance from spring's first thaw to
the onset of winter. The scents engulf you—
sweet and spicy, aromatic and bitter. The
air, laden with nature's infinite perfumes, is a
pleasure to breathe.

Let your nose lead you to the deep, organic
smells of the last uncut forest in the city—forty
acres of hemlock, oak, maple and hickory
(some trees more than two hundred fifty
years old) crisscrossed with mulch-covered
trails. There's a serene conifer forest, too;
giant evergreens tower above a penetrating bed
of balsamic pine needles—perhaps life's most
wistful essence.

There are so many pleasurable scents
emanating from the Botanical Garden,
you'll want to arrive early and leave late.
It's the only way to fully inhale New York's
most ambrosial experience.

The
New York
Earth Room

Address: 141 Wooster St.
(one block south of Houston St.)
Phone: 473-8072
Hours: Wednesday through Saturday,
Noon to 6 P.M.;
closed June to September
Admission: Free
Subway: N or R to Prince St.,
walk west to Wooster
Bus: M1, 6 (Broadway) to Prince St.

here's the dirt: One of the most pristine yet peculiar sanctuaries in New York is a SoHo loft filled with 280,000 pounds of topsoil.

The Earth Room is the creation of artist Walter De Maria, a reserved man who has little to say about his humble earth sculpture. It is difficult to survey this inert, silent scene for more than a few minutes, however, without concluding that it is a powerful statement about city life—or more

correctly, about the absence of pastoral
simplicity in our lives.

After the requisite exclamations of disbelief,
you'll sink into the disarming vibrations
of this austere space, empty except for the
3,600 square feet of wall-to-wall soil and a
few mushrooms. Settle down behind the low
Plexiglas partition so that the huge expanse
of earth is at eye level. Breathe in the sweet
smell and cool moisture of the rich black
loam. Plunge your hands into the soil.
Listen as the good earth reminds you it
always lies softly underfoot, a healing
cushion too easily forgotten in a city where
an impenetrable concrete crust separates you
from Nature's own terra firma below.

Outside of a few regulars who revive
themselves weekly at this friendly, fallow field,
you can call the Earth Room your own.
Just don't pick the mushrooms.

New York Public Library and Bryant Park

Address: 42nd St. bet. Fifth and Sixth Aves.
Phone: 340-0849
Hours: Library open Monday, Thursday,
Friday, Saturday 10 A.M. to 6 P.M.;
Tuesday and Wednesday, 11 A.M. to 7:30 P.M.
Park open daily 8:00 A.M. to Dusk
Admission: Free
Subway: 4, 5, 6 to Grand Central Station,
walk west
Bus: M1, 2, 3, 4 (Fifth and Madison Aves.)
to 42nd St.; M42 (42nd St. crosstown)
to Fifth Ave.

What's so special about a public library?

Well, this is not just any library, this is New York's Big Library. And after a five year, nine million dollar renovation, it also has a lush green carpet running the length of its backyard. So whether you go to see the lions, Patience and Fortitude, who guard the front entrance, or the imposing architecture, or the splendid exhibits, you'll be treated to

plenty of peace and quiet here. You just
have to know where to look.

While the vast main reading room on the third
floor (room 315) is somewhat noise free, even
greater seclusion exists just down the hall in
room 313, Art and Architecture. Provided you
peruse the books within, no one will bother
you. Feel a bit more daring? Finagle a pass to
one of the private study rooms such as room
320, the Berg Collection, where you'll find
ancient volumes on arcane subjects—and
absolute silence.

Once you feel properly edified inside, go out
back to the library's six-acre masterpiece of a
make-over; Bryant Park, designed by Lynden
B. Miller, has been transformed from a spooky
tangle of drug-infested hedges into a sweet,
secure, superbly-conceived city park that
encourages mindless rest and relaxation. And,
nobody has stolen the lawn chairs.

Nicholas Roerich Museum

Address: 319 West 107th St.
bet. Broadway and Riverside Dr.
Phone: 864-7752
Hours: Tuesday through Sunday, 2 to 5 P.M.
Admission: Free
Subway: 1, 9 to 110th St, walk south
Bus: M5, M104 to 107th St.

a trek through the Himalayan foothills is often characterized as the ultimate spiritual journey—as close as you can get to God and heaven with your feet still on the ground. If neither your schedule nor your budget permit a Himalayan expedition soon, a vicarious trek through the nearby Nicholas Roerich Museum might prove a good substitute.

This little known treasury contains almost 100 paintings by the Russian-born Roerich (1874-1947), a mystical artist and author who lived in the Himalayas for much of his life.

Respected internationally for his efforts to promote peace through culture, Roerich was also nominated for the Nobel Peace Prize in 1929. The casual town house dedicated to his work and spirit is furnished parlor style to encourage leisurely, deliberate viewing of his expansive mountain scenes.

It is difficult to describe the intensity of Roerich's landscape paintings except to say that they uplift you. On his illuminating canvases—rich with tempera blues, whites, violets, and reds—you are carried on a cloud to the roof of the world.

There is not a disappointing painting on the entire three floors of this blissful brownstone, but if you really want your soul to fly, proceed to Kanchenjunga (front room, second floor). It'll send you to another realm.

Open Center
Meditation Room

Address: 83 Spring St.
bet. Broadway and Crosby St.
Phone: 219-2527
Hours: Daily, 10 A.M. to 6 P.M.
Admission: Free
Subway: N or R to Prince St.; 6 to Spring St.
Bus: M1, 6 (Broadway) to Spring St.

the Open Center is the largest urban holistic center in the world, offering hundreds of fascinating courses for exploring consciousness, creativity, and spirit. The Center's catalog describes it as a "space into which we can withdraw from routine preoccupations," and people of all ages have found a supportive and healing environment here.

While the Center holds many attractions, my favorite is on the second floor where you'll find a room dedicated exclusively to private meditation. The incense-laden peace of this space has been enhanced by a blessing from an esteemed Tibetan lama. Also take note of the mottled rose and lilac–colored walls, the work of architectural painter, John Stolfo, who was commissioned by the Center to apply his "Lazure" painting technique (based on the teachings of Rudolf Steiner) to the room. Using natural-based, non-toxic paints combined with essential healing oils, Stolfo created rhythmic patterns on the walls intended to help meditators drop deeper into their contemplative experience. I've serenity-sampled the room both before and after the mood-altering paint job, and was impressed by the subtle difference.

The Open Center's meditation room offers a comforting place to pause during the day. On your way out be sure to stop by the bookstore on the first floor where you'll find a unique collection of holistic and spiritual books, New Age music, and workshop tapes.

Paley Park

Address: 53rd St.
bet. Fifth and Madison Aves.
Hours: Monday through Saturday,
8 A.M. to 7:45 P.M.
Admission: Free
Subway: E or F to Fifth Ave/53rd St.
Bus: M1, 2, 3, 4
(Fifth and Madison Aves.) to 53rd St.

this is not a park by suburban standards, but in midtown Manhattan you take whatever refuge you can get. An almost invisible oasis, Paley Park is situated in a concrete canyon between two biggish buildings, complete with a cascading twenty-five-foot waterfall.

Designed so visitors have to step away from the continuity of the street line to enter the park, its offering of serenity is most fully appreciated when you walk past the potted junipers and approach the waterfall.

When you sit on the stone steps facing the falls, virtually all city sounds are muted by the resonant rumbling of the cascade. Add the visual play of the water to make the experience deeply soothing and tranquilizing.

There's a small lighted niche on each side of the falls that's easily accessible and particularly secluded. With a refreshing mist bubbling up from the narrow catchment, I have always found that nestling there intensifies the sense of calm.

Noontime Note:
There are a concession stand and patio-type
furniture in the park to accommodate
business people and their picnic lunches.
Between noon and 2 P.M. on nice days,
it tends to get crowded. Skip those hours
and you'll avoid a busy, although not
unpleasant midday scene.

The **Paramount Hotel** Lobby

**Address: 235 West 43rd Street
bet. Broadway and Eighth Aves.
Phone: 764-5500
Hours: Daily, 24 hours
Admission: Free
Subway: A, C, E, 1, 9 , N, R to 42nd St.
Bus: M10 (Seventh and Eighth Aves.) to 42nd St.**

If you want to get technical, hotel lobbies are not exactly public domain since they exist primarily for the comfort and service of their guests. But in practice, anyone who has spent time in this city can tell you of a favorite hotel lobby where he or she goes to meet friends and business associates, make a phone call, gather thoughts before an important meeting, or simply cop some quick relief from a city that can get in your face.

Good hotel lobbies are often easier to find than the best public atriums, and unless you are a

particularly wacky dresser, or drag all your
worldly possessions around in a grocery cart,
you will not be asked to explain your
presence there.

For me, one hotel lobby stands out above the
rest—The Paramount. This fanciful space
designed by Philippe Starck is just so cool.
I love the hug-your-body-in-bold-velvet lounge
chairs, the gray Venetian walls, the shadowy
lighting, the overhanging mezzanine restaurant.
You might even bump into a Saturday Night
Live host ("accommodations for tonight's
guests provided by ...").

I duck into other hotel lobbies for refuge, too.
The Grand Hyatt (42nd Street and Lexington
Avenue) offers a quick escape from the noisy
netherworld of Grand Central Station. The very
upscale Four Seasons Hotel (57th Street
between Park and Madison Avenues) has simple
but elegant seating near the vaulted entranceway.

The Petrel

Address: Southeast corner of Battery Park
Phone: 825-1976
Hours: Several sails daily, mid-May through
mid-October (call for departure times)
Admission: $10 per person for midday sail,
$20 to $22 per person for sunset sail
Subway: R to Battery Park; 4, 5, 6 to Bowling
Green; 1 to South Ferry
Bus: M6 (Broadway) to State St.

Surrounded by concrete and steel in the gray canyons of Manhattan, it's easy to forget that we're living on an island. And islands are surrounded by water—big bodies of languorous liquid just perfect for sailing. The people at The Petrel haven't forgotten, and they can remind you, too, on the handsome teak decks of their seventy-six-foot yacht.

Designed by Sparkman and Stephens and named after the seabirds that fly farthest from land, The Petrel offers a unique opportunity to sail on a swift, powerful racing yacht through New York Harbor's protected and relatively calm waters. While reservations are suggested, it's often possible to walk down to The Petrel's incongruous dockside shanty at the tip of Battery Park and climb right aboard a scheduled sail. This is particularly true of the relaxing lunchtime cruises which last about forty-five minutes and offer plenty of sea spray and fun.

Once owned by the Coast Guard Academy and favored for sailing by John F. Kennedy during his presidency, this 1938 all-wood vessel skims through the waters of the lower harbor providing unparalleled views of old Manhattan and the Big Green Lady. On calm days, Captain Nick and his crew might even let you assist in a sailing maneuver— always challenging with a ninety-foot mainmast and 3000 square feet of sail. It's a friendly group down at The Petrel, eager to make this offshore mini-vacation an exhilarating Big Apple breeze.

Poets
House

Address: 72 Spring St.
bet. Crosby and Lafayette Sts., 2nd floor
Phone: 431-7920
Hours: Tuesday through Friday, 11:00 A.M. to
7:00 P.M.; Saturday, 11:00 A.M. to 4:00 P.M.;
Closed Sunday
Admission: Free
Subway: N or R to Prince St.; 6 to Spring St.
Bus: M1, 6 (Broadway) to Spring St.

the French essayist and moralist, Joseph Joubert, once wrote, "You will not find poetry anywhere unless you bring some of it with you."

Actually, he was only partially correct. You'll find lots of poetry, for instance, at the Poets House, even if you leave yours at home. In fact, the friendly staff has filled this comfortable, quiet, airy loft with more than 30,000 volumes of poetry. The collection is one of the largest in the country that is open to the public.

Poetry has been enjoying a popular resurgence, treated like newly discovered performance art on MTV and at local cafe readings. It's even showing up on city buses and subways as part of the "Poetry In Motion" program, not to mention regular readings on NPR. The power of poetry is nothing new to the people at the Poets House, where they've been "well-versed" in promoting the value and richness of poetry since 1985 when poets Stanley Kunitz and Elizabeth Kray founded this sanctuary for sonnets and refuge for rhyme. Today it is an important literary resource center and a meeting place for poets worldwide.

Bathed in sunlight streaming in through several floor-to-ceiling windows, and tastefully furnished with colorfully upholstered reading chairs, the Poets House is more a cozy living room than stuffy library. There is great respect for poetcraft here, and everyone is welcome.

The Quad at Columbia University

Address: 116th St. and Broadway
Hours: Daily, 8 A.M. to 6 P.M.
Admission: Free
Subway: 1, 9 to 116th St.
Bus: M4, M11, M104
(Broadway) to 116th St.

Leaving the tumult of Broadway to wander into the main quad at Columbia is like transferring from the schoolroom of urban survival to a restful course in personal revival.

The safest grounds in New York (big league security for busy Ivy Leaguers) are also a mecca for academic activity and reclusive repose. There's no need to worry about your age or how you're dressed, either—people just assume you're a graduate student or an esteemed university professor strolling the quad.

Relaxation 101 is self-taught every day in front of the Low Library, where you can nestle against the easternmost corner of that noble twelve-foot wall. It's a warm, windless nook excellent for studying the campus goings-on. Carry a book—cerebral reading is a popular pastime for all who recline on the broad lawns.

You might prefer the smaller, less-frequented quad in front of Uris Hall (look for the twisted black tubes called the "Curl" sculpture). Or amble through the maze of century-old buildings until you find your own solitary spot. There are a dozen on this postcard-perfect campus where you can partake of the scholarly atmosphere undisturbed.

My final evaluation: the Columbia quad is a high-spirited, unhurried place for intellectual and physical renewal. I give it an A.

Rumbul's
Back Room

Address: 20 Christopher St.
bet. Greenwich and Seventh Aves.
Phone: 924-8900
Hours: Daily, 9 A.M. to 1 A.M.
Admission: Sandwiches, desserts, coffee,
tea from $1
Subway: A, D, E, F to West 4th St.
Bus: M2, 3, 4, 5 to 9th St., walk west

What is it about a fireplace that can turn a difficult day into a forgiving one, or make an uncertain world seem less frightening? It's a question best considered in front of a blazing winter hearth, a light snow falling, and a cup of hot chamomile tea held securely between your hands.

I don't have a fireplace in my apartment, but they do down at Rumbul's—a good one, too, with a charred brick face, a stack of chunky hardwoods alongside, and the sound of crackling logs thawing the air. This is a fine, secluded place to snuggle with a friend, where the tea is served piping hot and you can watch the first snowflakes fall in the backyard garden.

I warm my toes at two other quaint Village eateries during the cold months. The Ye Waverly Inn (16 Bank Street and Waverly Place) is an 1844 carriage house with cozy wooden booths, wide floorboards, and two flickering fireplaces—try the chicken pot pie. You can also watch the flames dance at La Lanterna (129 McDougal Street at West 3rd Street), a true European style cafe where the cappuccino's strong and they sometimes forget you're there for hours.

Maybe I'll see you in the back room at Rumbul's some wintry day. Keep a log on the fire for me.

Russian & Turkish Baths

Address: 268 East Tenth St.,
bet. First Ave. and Ave. A
Phone: 674-9250
Hours: 9 A.M. to 10 P.M. (Monday, Tuesday,
Friday, Saturday—coed; Thursday and
Sunday—men only; Wednesday—women only)
Admission: $19 per day, all day
Subway: 6 to Astor Place, walk east
Bus: M15 (First and Second Aves.)
to Tenth St., walk east

the owner's name is Boris; the immigrant patrons kibbitz in Yiddish; and the kitchen serves a traditional borscht.

C★

This is the Russian & Turkish Baths (simply called the Tenth St. Baths by its devoted clientele), as authentic an Old World bathhouse as you're likely to find anywhere. Occupying the same Lower Eastside brownstone since 1892, this temple of sweat is not for the delicate, the pampered, or the fanatically clean. Funkiness is what gives this place its decidedly offbeat charm, and probably what keeps the trendy crowds away.

Bring a bathing suit for coed days (this place is straight), then head downstairs to the nostril-burning Russian room (dry heat), the Turkish room (wet heat), the cold plunge, and the Swedish shower. The Russian room seems to be everybody's favorite kiln, and once you recover from the initial fear of having all your body fluids boil out your ears, you begin to appreciate the palpable feeling of tension melt. For an extra fee you can have a platza—a traditional head-to-toe thrashing with an oak leaf broom.

Give yourself plenty of "schvitzing" time here, because you'll also want to spend at least an hour lounging on an upstairs bunk bed. I've had my most rejuvenating, transcendental dozes in the half state following the intense sweat purge of the Baths. An all-day stay just might put you in a permanently blissful state of Jell-O.

st. Luke's Garden

Address: Hudson St. bet. Barrow and Grove Sts.
Hours: Monday through Friday, 8 A.M. to 7 P.M.;
Saturday and Sunday, 8 A.M. to 4 P.M.
Admission: Free
Subway: 1, 9 to Sheridan Square, walk west
Bus: M10 (Seventh and
Eighth Aves.) to Christopher St.

for anyone who grew up in the suburbs, one
of the great memories of childhood
was having a backyard.

You knew there was a fast-paced world rushing
past your front door, but out back life was
easy and innocent and fun. The backyard was a
faraway place to hide in a daydream, to stare at
the sky, or to simply forget.

St. Luke's Garden is the closest thing to having
your own backyard in New York City. In fact, it
actually is the backyard for several handsome

nineteenth century brownstones that enclose the secret garden on two sides. For years I'd peer behind the wall at St. Luke's, envious of whoever had access to this apparently private spot. Turns out all my peering was pointless; the obscured public gate wasn't far away. You enter this green oasis by passing under the gold and white sign on Hudson Street that reads "St. Luke's School." Follow the footpath west, then south through the quaint schoolyard until you reach the welcoming garden gate.

Splendidly concealed behind an ivy-blanketed brick wall, the garden feels well-removed from the Village activity which surrounds it. The mandala-like design of its stone pathways and the thoughtfully placed magnolia-hidden benches contribute to a sense of privacy. St. Luke's Garden is a neat retreat in winter, too, when its dormant foliage is a study in tones of gray, brown, green and red.

St. Patrick's Cathedral

Address: Fifth Ave. bet. 50th and 51st Sts.
Phone: 753-2261
Hours: Daily, 6:30 A.M. to 8:45 P.M.
Admission: Free
Subway: E, F to 53rd St.; B, D, F to
Rockefeller Center
Bus: M1, 2, 3, 4, and 18
(Fifth and Madison Aves.) to 50th St.

new York has so many magnificent churches, synagogues, and religious centers, all conducive to inner contemplation and quiet, it is difficult to single out just one.

St. Patrick's Cathedral would certainly have to be counted among the most beautiful, however, with its twin Gothic spires rising 330 feet above the street. The cathedral's cavernous interior seats 2400 people, houses an organ with more than 7380 pipes, and contains some of the most breathtaking stained glass in the world.

You don't have to be searching for salvation
to benefit from the cathedral's ready gift of
peace and quiet. With acres of polished
wooden pews, there is always an isolated corner
in which to escape. I particularly enjoy the
altars to saints which you'll find by walking past
the pulpit at the east end of the cathedral.
I'm always amazed to find so much solitude
just steps from Fifth Avenue, and smack
in the middle of Manhattan.

For those who can't conveniently get to
midtown, I think you'll find these other
spiritual sanctuaries to be equally sustaining:
Grace Church (Broadway at 10th Street),
the Cathedral of St. John the Divine
(West 112th Street and Amsterdam Avenue),
Temple Emanu-El (Fifth Avenue and 65th
Street), and Trinity Church (Broadway
and Wall Street).

Snug Harbor
Cultural Center

Address: 1000 Richmond Terrace, Staten Island
Phone: (718) 448-2500
Hours: Daily, 9 A.M. to 5 P.M.
Admission: Free
Bus: From Staten Island Ferry, take S40
directly to Snug Harbor (two miles)
Auto: Verrazano Bridge (lower level), to first
exit on Bay St., to Snug Harbor

Whenever I'm at Snug Harbor, I catch myself glancing around for leathery-faced guys with peg legs and eye patches. This former retirement community for "aged, decrepit, and worn out sailors" hasn't served that function in many years; it's just that the entire eighty acres of parklands, Greek Revival buildings and Victorian cottages look so much like they did back in the 1830s.

Snug Harbor was purchased by the City of New York in 1976, but the restoration of its buildings has slowed with the economy—and that has left this relic of a nautical era in less than perfect condition. Still, the nationally landmarked historic district overlooking New York Bay is a fascinating place to explore.

For a delightfully creepy experience, walk down the old funeral march road (Cottage Row) where deceased sailors were escorted to their graves. You can follow this processional path to remote sections of the wooded grounds, too, then loop back past a large pond lined with willows, wetlands, and the English-style perennial gardens of the Staten Island Botanical Society. Snug Harbor remains a bit of a buried treasure, a well-kept secret from both sea and land-bound publics. Even if you're not an old salt, do set sail for historic Snug Harbor.

Traveler's Note: As a fast growing center for the arts, Snug Harbor offers a year-round program of concerts, dance recitals, art exhibits, and workshops. Call ahead for a current schedule.

South Cove

Address: South End Ave. at Battery Park City
Hours: Daily, 24 hours
Admission: Free
Subway: A, C, E to World Trade Center,
walk west
Bus: M10 (Eighth Ave.) to Battery Park City

Whenever I approach this playful inlet, it begins to work its primal magic, reminding me instantly how much and how often I long to be near water.

It is not surprising that South Cove should have this effect, since everything about it—from the boulder-studded boardwalk and bowed bridge to the arching jetty and crown-like observation deck—is designed to get people back to the shoreline. For decades the Hudson waterfront here was rendered inaccessible by a frustrating barrier of decaying wharves and razor-topped fences. Reclaiming this neglected

landscape for refuge-starved New Yorkers
is precisely what artists and architects
had uppermost in their minds when they
conceived South Cove.

You can see, smell, even feel the surge
of the river from any point along the curving
architecture of this sheltered recess. The
harmonic sounds of its swirling eddies beckon
you to the water's edge. And the three-acre
coastal park overflows with sunny seats,
too; try out the rail-tie benches against the
south-facing wall which stay cozily warm
even in winter.

The extremely safe, always quiet South Cove
reveals its most compelling feature at night,
when cobalt blue ship's lanterns turn the nook
into a romantic fantasyland. This is the
precious, whispering light of the heart—
bring along a special friend.

Strawberry Fields

Address: Central Park West at 72nd St.
Hours: Daily, 24 hours
Admission: Free
Subway: B or C to 72nd St.
Bus: M10 (Seventh and Eighth Aves.) to 72nd
St.; M72 (72nd St. crosstown)
to Central Park West

at the entrance to Strawberry Fields, a sign reads Reserved for Quiet Recreation. While New Yorkers may be less than fanatical in their observance of these posted notices, their devotion to Beatle's icon John Lennon is quite another matter.

Located across the street from the Dakota, where Yoko Ono still resides, this four-and-a-half-acre living memorial to Lennon created by his wife seems to be permanently imbued with the spirit of the Sixties. Once you step over the black and white "Imagine" mosaic embedded

in the footpath leading to Strawberry Fields,
you feel just a bit more hopeful—much
as we did back then.

The first thing you'll notice about this idyllic
setting is that it's scrupulously cared for,
thanks to the private funds earmarked for its
upkeep. Sun-dappled and friendly in every
season, planted flower beds and grassy knolls
receive daily, almost constant attention.

You won't have any trouble finding
breathing space here, but you can treat
yourself to a particularly quieting experience
by walking to the northernmost end of the
upper lawn where it comes to an abrupt point.
See that single redwood tree in front of the
hedge line? Under that tree I fed a sparrow
a piece of bread from my hand.
Imagine.

Sutton Place Park

Address: Sutton Place at 57th St.
Hours: Daily, 24 hours
Admission: Free
Subway: 4, 5, 6 to 59th St., walk east
Bus: M15 (First and Second Aves.) to 57th
St.; M57 (57th St. crosstown)

the most rejuvenating urban parks are those with a distinct feeling of detachment from the noise and turbulence of the city.

❧

The physical design of Sutton Place Park makes it just such a soothing setting. A three-foot retaining wall and an eight-foot drop from street level completely conceal this park from Sutton Place and 57th Street. But it's there, tucked between a stately brownstone and a tall residential building. Just descend the switch-back ramp and you'll enter a friendly and protected realm.

At first, your gaze settles on Porcellino, the life-sized wild boar (a replica of a beloved bronze sculpture in Florence, Italy) who patiently and imposingly presides over this quiet park. Next, your eyes are drawn to the movement of the East River—the park's visual focal point. If you stand near the edge of the quadrangle and look down, you have the feeling you're suspended over swirling waters. This evokes the pleasant sensation of riding atop the river currents, and lures the mind away from outer-world intrusions.

⁓

Sutton Place is one of the city's most exclusive neighborhoods and as a result, its park enjoys excellent police protection. Visitors here are composed and respectful, the atmosphere is sedate, and you'll ascend the ramp to the real world with renewed equanimity.

Synchro
Energize

Address: 594 Broadway, Suite 905
(just south of Houston St.)
Phone: 941-1184
Hours: Daily, Noon to 9 P.M., by appt.
Admission: Session, $20 for 45 minutes
Subway: N or R to Prince St.
Bus: M1, 6 (Broadway) to Prince St.

S ynchro Energize is one of the weirdest and most psychedelic experiences I've ever had. It's also one of the most deeply meditative and rejuvenating.

Synchro Energize calls itself New York's only brain-mind fitness center. In this pleasant SoHo loft, a powerful combination of light, sound and electromagnetics promotes "whole brain integration"—a kind of forced relaxation state tripped off when your right and left hemispheres come into greater synchrony.

The process is simple. You lie on a futon mat or water bed, don goggles lined with pulsating white lights, and listen to synchronized nature sounds or New Age music. After a few unsettling moments, you begin to relax. Forty-five minutes later, you feel completely calm, yet energized.

During my first visit, I actually experienced a sort of time collapse—my 45-minute session felt like ten minutes. I also remember conjuring up all sorts of original geometric patterns and colors. I thought I'd become an artistic genius until I discovered I couldn't reproduce any of my visions once the session ended.

Regular clients claim benefits ranging from reduced fears and memory improvement to normalized sleep patterns and enhanced creativity. All I know is, Synchro Energize gives me a greater sense of well-being.

The Terrace at Blue Cross Center

Address: 622 Third Ave. at 40th St.
Hours: Daily, 8 A.M. to 5:30 P.M. (seasonal)
Admission: Free
Subway: 4, 5, 6, 7 to Grand Central Station,
walk southeast
Bus: M101 (Third and Lexington Aves.)
to 40th St.

i don't think it's accidental that the people at Blue Cross Blue Shield open their serene, second-floor terrace to the public. After all, who should take a greater interest in the stress-reducing benefits of a peaceful sanctuary than the state's largest health insurance company?

For years I passed beneath this hedge-lined terrace assuming it was a private patio for Blue Cross employees only. I was wrong. When I found the unmarked access stairs and escalators (40th Street, just west of Third Avenue),

I discovered I could go right up.
There's nothing fancy about this hidden terrace,
just plenty of comfortable molded chairs,
nine whispering trees, good security, and very
few people—all twenty feet above the street.
It's the perfect prescription for urban sanity.

You can enjoy a quiet brown bag lunch among
the uniquely-shaped "mushroom" tables, or
tilt your head back and gaze into the patch
of dizzying sky framed by five office
buildings looming above. This induces a
delightful state of self-hypnosis.

Keep this place in mind as an unadorned,
yet always reliable escape from the stresses of
midtown. Think of a visit here as a simple form
of preventive medicine—and one that won't add
a penny to your health care costs.

United Nations Garden

Address: First Ave. at 45th St.
Phone: 963-1234
Hours: Daily, 9 A.M. to 5:30 P.M.
Admission: Free; no food or drink allowed
Subway: 4, 5, 6 to Grand Central, walk east
Bus: M15 (First and Second Aves.) to 42nd
St.; M42 (42nd St. crosstown)
to First Ave.

While the United Nations is a favorite stop for foreign tourists, New Yorkers routinely overlook this monument to global brotherhood. Look again, because just north of the UN's celebrated glass and concrete buildings is an expansive, under-utilized garden providing the perfect urban getaway.

Within the UN's sixteen acres of grounds and garden, you'll find 1400 prize-winning rosebushes, 185 flowering cherry trees, fifty-two dwarf fruit trees, plus ambling walkways,

strategically placed benches, and a half-mile
paved esplanade offering spectacular views of
the East River. This is truly a walkway of the
world, with a mosaic of smiling faces from
almost every country on earth assuring you
that global peace is still possible. Guarded
by U.N. security, the area is also extremely safe.

Whenever I'm there, I quickly gravitate towards
the Eleanor Roosevelt Memorial in the northeast
corner of the garden. It's tucked away behind a
small stand of trees and from the seclusion of its
huge stone bench you can while away an entire
afternoon. Or even doze undisturbed. I have.

*Note: Be sure to see the twisted pistol sculpture
at the 45th Street entrance to the garden.
How safe our city would be if every firearm
looked as useless as this one.*

Water Street Plaza

Address: 55 Water St. at Old Slip Rd.
Hours: Daily, 24 hours
Admission: Free
Subway: N, R to Whitehall St.,
walk east
Bus: M15 (First and Second
Aves.) to South Ferry

during my research for this book, a friend
told me about an elevated public plaza in the
financial district that is virtually unknown.
I realized he was onto something when it
took me three visits to find it.

Water Street Plaza is not well marked at
ground level which ensures its relative privacy.
From the Staten Island Ferry terminal, head
northeast up Water Street to the sidewalk
monolith bearing the ten Chemical Bank
logos. About thirty feet before you reach the
monolith look to your right. See that bank

of escalators marked "Plaza Level" squeezed between the building walls? It appears they ascend directly into the office buildings above, but actually they usher you up to an enormous brick plaza—an open space that's all yours.

The best vantage point is the eastern-facing upper terrace looking out on the Brooklyn boat yards and Governor's Island. You'll find benches placed here for optimal sun exposure and prime river viewing, with no more than a handful of neighborhood office workers sitting along them. Also note the southeast steps leading to the Vietnam Veterans Memorial. You'll be moved by its evocative, glass-brick "letter wall."

My friend asked me not to mention that Water Street Plaza is also the most private place in the district to watch East River fireworks. Oops.

Wave Hill

Address: 675 West 252nd St., Bronx
Phone: (718) 549-3200
Hours: Tuesday through Sunday 10 A.M. to
5:30 P. M. (4:30 P.M. Winter);
closed Monday
Admission: Free weekdays, $4 weekends
Subway/Bus: Call for directions
Auto: Henry Hudson Pkwy. to 246-250th St.,
north to 252nd St., follow signs to Wave Hill

Ladies and gentlemen, may I present your country estate.

❧

All right, all right, not *your* country estate, but *a* country estate, and you're invited to come up here anytime you like and use it.

❧

Managed by the city, Wave Hill in the Riverdale section of the Bronx has been lovingly restored to a time when former owners Teddy Roosevelt, Mark Twain, and Arturo Toscanini called it their weekend retreat. Today it offers nature-deprived cityfolk a congenial and florid escape just fifteen minutes drive from Manhattan. The twenty-eight acres of glorious gardens, quaint greenhouses, sweeping lawns, a lily pond, and unspoiled woodlands sit high atop a hill overlooking the Hudson. From here you're face-to-face with a geologic wonder that never disappoints—the Palisades.

The former mansion residence contains a gift shop and cafe on the main level, with a children's environmental education center in the basement (check out the beehive with fresh honey off the comb). There's also plenty of clean air and open land at Wave Hill and lots of inviting spots to turn your back on a tight and toxic city. Many gravitate toward the rough-hewn gazebo in the wild garden, but I'm partial to the high-backed lawn chairs generously distributed throughout the grounds. Sitting there, Wave Hill just might inspire you to dig out the old paintset.

World Financial Center

**Address: West Street, just west of the World
Trade Center, at the Hudson River
Phone: 945-0505
Hours: Daily, 6 A.M. to Midnight
Admission: Free
Subway: 1, R, N, A, E to World Trade Center,
follow signs to World Financial Center
Bus: M10 (7th and 8th Aves.)
to Battery Park City**

If you've always considered the pursuit of money to be contradictory to the pursuit of peace and quiet, you should invest a little time at the World Financial Center.

Here, the financial barons of Wall Street have spent oodles of money on a wharf-like mall that is not only spectacular to look at, but also is purposefully designed to be a haven for frazzled money managers. (Of course, they're all supposed to be too busy to use it; why let their investment go to waste.)

Here are my three favorite spots: 1. the pink granite benches below and in front of the "quotation" fence facing the cove (you'll know it when you see it); 2. the circle of wooden benches in the maze garden at the southeast corner of the mall; and 3. the broad promenade that begins at the southwest corner of the cove. Although not technically part of the Financial Center, this bench-lined walkway which extends nearly to Battery Park has river views and romance to rival Paris. It's well lit and safe at night, too.

The Winter Garden—a huge atrium with shops and exhibits—is undeniably impressive, but I find its echo chamber ambience oppressive. If you feel as I do, you might prefer to grab a snack inside and carry it outside to one of the recommended locations.

About
the Author

Allan Ishac is an award-winning advertising copywriter and scriptwriter for the best-selling children's video Real Life, Giant Construction Equipment for Kids. He is a recipient of the Mayor's Volunteer Superstars Award for his bedtime story readings at Beth Israel Hospital in New York. He lives in Manhattan.